SIGHT READING FOR MALLETS

Jazz Exercises in Even and Odd Times for Mallets and Other Instruments

by Emil Richards

ISBN 978-1-4234-6990-2

7777 W. BLUEMOUND RD. P.O. BOX 13819 MILWAUKEE, WI 53213

In Australia Contact:
Hal Leonard Australia Pty. Ltd.
4 Lentara Court
Cheltenham, Victoria, 3192 Australia
Email: ausadmin@halleonard.com.au

Visit Hal Leonard Online at
www.halleonard.com

To Camille

CONTENTS

Introduction

As a film-studio musician for over thirty years, I have had the good fortune to play music written by the leading and most innovative movie composers, including John Williams, Bill Conti, Lalo Schifrin, Henry Mancini, Michael Kaimen, and Quincy Jones. I have also traveled and performed with such diverse artists as Frank Sinatra, Frank Zappa, George Harrison, George Shearing, Stan Kenton, Harry Partch, and Ravi Shankar.

Being able to sight read a wide variety of music, embracing virtually every musical style and format, has given me the opportunity to perform with these and other highly creative and successful musicians. In order to succeed as a recording, "show," or concert musician, you must be able to sight read. Since the beginning of my career I have read tons of music. And over the years, I continue to be asked two prime questions: *What can I do to improve my sight reading? What materials are available to help me?"*

I have written this book to help anyone who is sincerely interested in improving his or her sight reading abilities. For this book I have composed a series of compositions that utilize rhythmic, melodic, and harmonic situations that you will encounter throughout your musical career. I hope that these exercises will help you improve your sight reading, and that this book will become a valuable part of your musical library.

Sight reading is not a gift, but a skill that can be learned and developed. Two associate skills that are essential to improving your sight reading are: **(1) Sight Singing.** By being able to actually sing and pre-hear what is written you will be able to internalize the music, and your sight reading will become more fluid and confident. **(2) Theoretical Analysis.** Your ability to quickly analyze and mentally process the music will help to increase your speed and accuracy. Sight reading is the syntheses of a variety of skills and knowledge.

While written primarily for the mallet player, any instrumentalist may profit from the study of these compositions. The pieces containing four-note chords should be played as written by mallet, guitar, and keyboard players; other instrumentalists should play the lead or top note of each chord cluster.

You will note that in the "Guide to the Comositions" section that metronomic markings have been given. I suggest that the very first time that you play each composition, you try sight reading it at the designated tempo, without stopping. Then before trying the piece again, go back and read the "Guide" for that composition. These compositions contain a multitude of rhythmic phrases and odd-time groupings that you will want to ponder and become familiar with. Because of the complexity of each composition, you should go over them slowly many times so that you hear and really "see" the rhythmic, melodic, and harmonic elements and structure of each piece.

When I see a new piece of music, I always approach it in a systematic way. First, I glance over it to identify "familiar" phrases and patterns. Then, I put my focus on any new or unusual phrases, rhythms, and groupings that require special attention and a greater amount of concentration to play. You should condition yourself to be able to mentally hear and conceptualize the music before you actually play it.

In addition to serving as tools to improve your sight reading I hope that you enjoy playing these exercises as original compositions offering richly diverse musical experiences and insights. Work hard, but have fun.

—Emil Richards

(I wish to thank Sanford Lung and Gerry James for preparing this text. Without their help I don't know how I could have finished.   —E.R.

GUIDE TO THE COMPOSITIONS

Page 8. **SHEEP LIE** ♩ = 104 Note the use of a sixteenth note followed by a dotted eighth note throughout this piece. Play the notation over a few times until it begins to feel comfortable.

Page 9. **SAME PHRASE DIFFERENT PLACE** ♩ = 120. Note the whole phrase is six bars long and is played four times, but appears in a different place in the bar each time.

Page 10. **INDO LATINO** ♩ = 84. If you play the first two bars over and over, alternating hands, you will find you are playing the basic *clavé* beat with your right hand and the reverse *clavé* with your left. The last eight bars contain what is called a *Te-Hi* in Indian music: a phrase played three times, the last beat of which ends on a down-beat of the ninth bar.

Page 11. **YO YAZZ** ♩ = 162. A blues in three quarter time with a slight variation. Each bar is twice as long, so the blues becomes twice as long (24 bars). Note the turn around bars, 17 – 20 use a variation of the chord structure conventionally used in the blues form.

Page 12. **HIMALAYA 5–0.** ♩ = 174. Two choruses of the Blues structure played in $5/4$ time. The accented bars are played $5/8$ twice in each measure.

Page 13. **SAKE SIPPIN** ♩ = 150. A piece in $7/4$. The break down is mostly a $3/4$ - $4/4$ in each measure. The next to the last two lines have two bars of $3/4$ followed by two bars of $4/4$ or a 14 beat phrase.

Page 14. **TRIPLE OCTAVE TRIPLETS** ♩ = 72. If you start with right hand sticking, this composition will lay comfortably. Note the two sixteenth notes that appear in different places within the $12/8$ feeling.

Page 15. **THE LONG BLUES** ♩ = 87. This blues in $4/4$ is twice as long as the standard 12 bars. Note the continued use of dotted eighth and sixteenth notes.

Page 16. **INTO SOMEWHERE** ♩. = 92 This composition is written in $6/8$: six equal eighth notes **not** triplets. The first and second endings are ten bars long. Note that the accented bars are a feeling of four inside the six.

Page 17. **I GOT SOMPIN** ♩ = 156 or ♪ = 312. Give this $^7/_8$ composition a feeling of 2-2-2-1 in the first two lines; line three a 4-3 feeling; line four, 5-5-4 over each two bars; lines five and six, 4-4-3-3. The remainder repeats the permutations.

Page 18. **ISADOR** ♪ = 224. The permutations used in the $^9/_8$ composition are 2-2-2-3 on the first line; 2-2-2-2-1 on the second line. Lines five and six are 3-3-3 or 2-1, 2-1, 2-1.

Page 19. **IT'S TEN TO FIVE** ♩ = 175 The $^{10}/_4$ is played 3-3-4. The $^5/_4$ in the last two lines is played 3-2.

Page 20. **LUCKY ELEVEN** ♩ = 182 This blues in $^{11}/_4$ is broken down as 3-3-5 or 3-3-3-2.

Page 21. **BOMBAY BOSSA** ♪ = 224 or ♩ = 112 This composition can be felt in $^{21}/_8$ or 10 $^{1/2}/_4$. Break it down as $^4/_4$-$^4/_4$-$^5/_8$. The last three lines are played double: four bars of $^4/_4$ and two bars of $^5/_8$.

Page 22. **BUTTER JUG WALTZ** ♩ = 150 The feeling of dotted eighth and sixteenth notes in extended phrases in $^3/_4$ time.

Page 23. **A DAILY FOG** ♩ = 154 Some of the beats push an eighth note before the down beat and other phrases play on the beat.

Page 24. **HOT FUDGE SUNDAY** ♩ = 140 Find (and play) the double stops in a $^5/_4$ feeling.

Page 25. **SOUR SALLY WHITE** ♪ = 280. Play this $^7/_8$ piece with a 3-2-2 feeling. Lines four and five have accents on 3-3-3-3-2. Line seven, 2-3 2-3 2-2 or 5-5-4.

Page 26. **CURRY** ♪ = 232 This $^{11}/_8$ composition can also be played in 5 $^{1/2}/_4$. Alternatively, from line three it is permutated as $^4/_4$-$^3/_8$.

Page 27. **THE DAY AFTER A NIGHT IN TUNISIA** ♩ = 126 Although the melody seems strange over the chord structures, they work!

Pages 28–29. **CYCLES** ♪ = 160 This $^{12}/_8$ composition moves the sixteenth note to different beats in every measure.

Pages 30–31. **WELL I DIDN'T** ♩ = 125 This piece utilizes the triplet with double sixteenth notes within. Lines three and four at page 31 show the use of the Double Diminished Scale moving around chromatically.

Page 32.   **DU DU** ♩ = 140 This $^3/_4$ composition in bar three has 4 equal beats within the $^3/_4$ measure. Think of accenting every three sixteenth notes. Line six has accents every 4th eighth note over a two bar phrase.

Page 33.   **DEJAVU** ♩ = 150 This $^5/_4$ piece utilizes the tritone ($^+$4th). Each bar plays a tonic and its corresponding tritone within each measure.

Page 34.   **GO-O-LLY** ♩ = 150 The use of double stops are used here with the melody being played in the left hand. This is a straight $^7/_4$ feeling until lines five and six where the accents switch to 3-3-3-3-2.

Page 35.   **ONCE THERE WERE NINE-TEENS** ♩ = 350 or ♩ = 175 The numbers above each measure show the breakdown of the $^{19}/_4$. Wherever the accents change, the numbers have been written above the group of 19 beats.

Page 36.   **TRUST FRIENDS** ♩ = 140 Notice the use of dotted eighths and sixteenths together with groups of triplets. Be sure to distinguish between them.

Page 37.   **ALEXANDRIA'S RAGA TIME BAND** ♩ = 162 This $^{13}/_4$ composition is divided $^3/_4$-$^3/_4$-$^3/_4$-$^4/_4$ and $^5/_4$-$^4/_4$-$^4/_4$.

Pages 38–39.   **SKIP ONE** ♩ = 156 This composition in $^{15}/_8$ has many permutations. It can be felt 7 $^{1/2}/_4$ or $^6/_4$ - $^3/_8$ or you can play three bars of $^5/_8$ to equal $^{15}/_8$ as in line four, or five bars of $^3/_8$ to equal $^{15}/_8$ as in line seven.

Pages 40–41.   **ENJOY** ♩ = 175 The first page is a feeling of a samba in $^3/_4$. The chords ascend in minor thirds every eight bars. The melody on page 41 mirrors the chords on page 40.

Pages 42–43.   **AMOS** ♩ = 175 This study combines major and minor thirds in a four-mallet chord structure. Note from line 6 on page 42 to the end of page 43 where the major and minor chords appear.

Page 44.   **BED SPRING** ♩ = 150 Notice the sequence of phrases that occur from lines one and two to lines three and four. The whole composition moves harmonically in sequential phrases.

Page 45.   **THE REAL RAD** ♩ = 88   This four-mallet study utilizes the 13th chord in a blues idiom. The melody remains the same while the harmony moves chromatically up and down.

1
SHEEP LIE

2
SAME PHRASE DIFFERENT PLACE

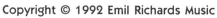

3
INDO LATINO

4
YO YAZZ

5

HIMALAYA-5-O

6
SAKE SIPPIN

13

7
TRIPLE OCTAVE TRIPLETS

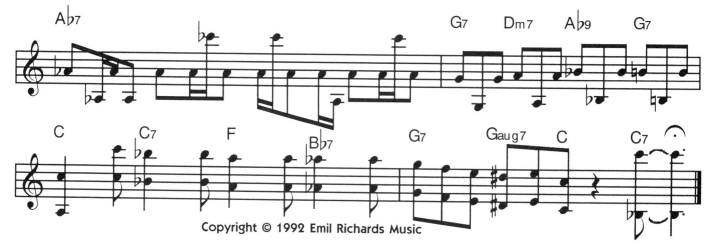

8

THE LONG BLUES

♩ = 87

9
INTO SOMEWHERE

10

I GOT SOMPIN

11
ISADOR

♪ = 224

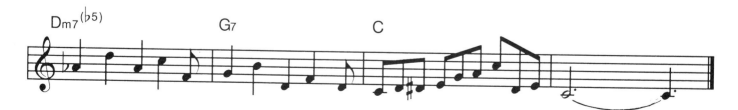

12

IT'S TEN TO FIVE

13

LUCKY ELEVEN

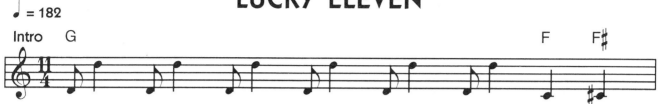

14

BOMBAY BOSSA

 = 224

15

BUTTER JUG WALTZ

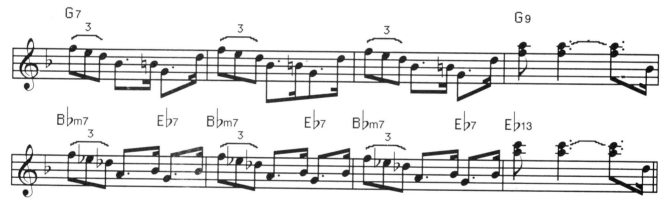

16

A DAILY FOG

♩ = 154

23

17

HOT FUDGE SUNDAY

♩ = 140

18

SOUR SALLY WHITE

♪ = 280

19

CURRY

♪ = 280
Intro

20

THE DAY AFTER A NIGHT IN TUNISIA

21
CYCLES

♪ = 160

22
WELL I DIDN'T

23

DU DU

24

DEJAVU

25

GO-O-LLY

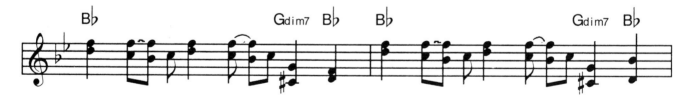

26

ONCE THERE WERE NINE-TEENS

27
TRUST FRIENDS

28

ALEXANDRIA'S RAGA TIME BAND

29

SKIP ONE

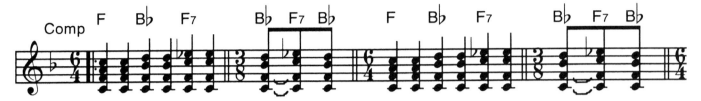

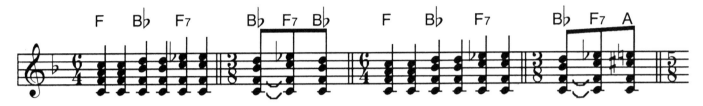

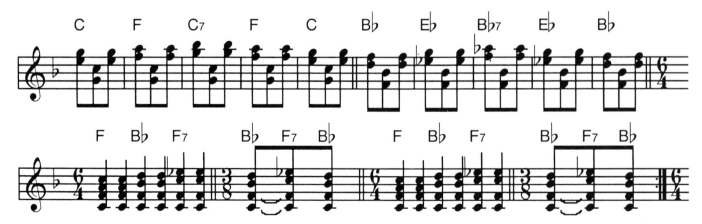

Melody

30

ENJOY

Comp

Melody

Last x only

31

AMOS

♩ = 175

BED SPRING

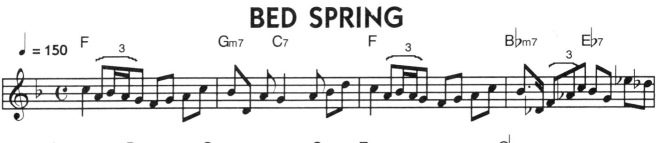

33

THE REAL RAD

MASTER YOUR MALLET TECHNIQUE
with Hal Leonard

EXERCISES FOR MALLET INSTRUMENTS
Musical Etudes for Two and Four Malletsand Other Instruments
by Emil Richards

Exercises for Mallet Instruments contains jazz licks in all keys, adapted from the music of Debussy, Ravel, Bartok, Stravinsky, John Coltrane, and Charlie Parker. Practicing these etudes over jazz chords changes is an invaluable addition to the techniques of improvisation, and will improve reading skills. These 500 studies, along with seven original songs, were designed with the mallet player in mind, but will benefit any instrumentalist.

06620132 . . . . $19.99

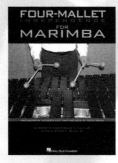

FOUR-MALLET INDEPENDENCE FOR MARIMBA
Progressive Studies for Two Mallets in Each Hand
by Johnny Lee Lane and Samuel A. Floyd, Jr.
edited by Richard L. Walker, Jr.

In this book, Johnny Lee Lane and Samuel A. Floyd, Jr. take you through a concentrated study of progressively arranged exercises. Through careful study and practice of the book's valuable musical examples, you will build a solid foundation in the independent manipulation of two mallets in each hand.

06620099 . . . . $9.95

FOUR-MALLET MARIMBA PLAYING
A Musical Approach for All Levels
by Nancy Zeltsman

This book contains a variety of music, from musical etudes designed for beginning and intermediate players, to recital material appropriate for intermediate and advanced marimbists. It includes: examples taken from contemporary solo and chamber works; 50 studies to develop four-mallet technique in a musical way; 18 classic and contemporary solos for recitals, auditions or juries; and helpful guidelines for mallet selection, grip, strokes, tone production, rolls, stickings, phrasing and other important topics.

06620055 . . . . $19.95

INTERMEDIATE PROGRESSIVE ETUDES
by David Kovins
The Vibraphone Virtuosity Series

This book/CD pack will help develop a contemporary vibist's technique and musicianship. It includes: 33 etudes in different styles; chromatic exercises; whole-tone scales; and studies in perfect fourths. It covers techniques such as: mallet dampening, pedaling, musical phrasing, and more. Each etude is performed on the accompanying disc, and some contain chord symbols to allow for improvisation.

06620026 Book/CD Pack $14.95

MALLET CHORD STUDIES
Chord Voicings and Arpeggio Patterns for Two and Four Mallets and Other Instruments
by Emil Richards

Mallet Chord Studies provides exercises that cover the open and closed positions found in most jazz phrasings on keyboard instruments. The etudes are designed to improve the improvisational skills needed to play all seventh chords in various open and closed positions. They will help the player to become proficient in moving from one chord and scale sequence to another. Though written primarily with mallet instrumentalists in mind, this practical book is suitable for any keyboard player.

06620134 . . . . $9.99

MELODY & RHYTHM PERMUTATIONS
More Than 300 Exercises for Mallets and Other Instruments
by Emil Richards

The exercises in *Melody & Rhythm Permutations* were developed to improve sight reading and improvisational skills in the advanced player. The inversions of melody and rhythm will keep the instrumentalist busy analyzing and performing these musical studies over the long haul, and a note from the author offers insights and practice suggestions. Though written primarily for mallet players, any instrumentalist will benefit from mastering these etudes.

06620135 . . . . $19.99

MODERN SCHOOL FOR XYLOPHONE, MARIMBA & VIBRAPHONE

This method features exercises and studies that cover the problems of technique in playing these instruments. Includes 30 progressive etudes, arrangements of violin concertos by Bach and Paganini for 'fixed-pitch' percussion, and orchestral excerpts from Ravel, Stravinsky, Shostakovich, Kabalevsky, Gershwin, Delibes, and others.

00347776 . . . . $12.95

SIGHT READING FOR MALLETS
by Emil Richards

As a long-time studio musician, Emil Richards knows the importance of sight reading and in this book has provided a superb source for those who would like to improve the skills needed to play today's music. *Sight Reading for Mallets* contains over 30 compositions that offer experience playing the unusual rhythms and phrases found in 21st-century writing. Though written primarily for mallets, any instrumentalist will gain the same benefits.

06620133 . . . . $12.99

VOICING AND COMPING FOR JAZZ VIBRAPHONE
by Thomas L. Davis

Here is the definitive guide to chordal playing for the contemporary vibraphonist. Includes material on: voicing selection, chord-member selection, use of extensions and alterations, voice leading, inversion selection, and more. The accompanying CD contains demos and play-along tracks with notated charts featuring standard chordal progressions in the following styles: fast & medium swing, ballad, jazz waltz, bossa-nova, and samba. This book is the most complete – and fun! – way to learn four-mallet voicings and comping patterns for jazz vibes.

06620019 Book/CD Pack $12.95

For more information, see your local music dealer, or write to:

HAL•LEONARD® CORPORATION
7777 W. BLUEMOUND RD. P.O. BOX 13819 MILWAUKEE, WI 53213

www.halleonard.com

Prices, contents, and availability subject to change without notice.

0509